I Like Bugs

The Sound of B

By Alice K. Flanagan

I like bugs.

Some bugs are big.

5

Some bugs are small.

Some bugs fly.

Some bugs crawl.

Some bugs
have six legs.

13

Some bugs
have lots
of legs.

Some bugs bite us.

17

18

Some bugs help us.

I like bugs.

20

Word List:

big

bite

bugs

Note to Parents and Educators

The books in this series are based on current research, which supports the idea that our brains are pattern-detectors rather than rules-appliers. This means children learn to read easier when they are taught the familiar spelling patterns found in English. As children encounter more complex words, they have greater success in figuring out these words by using the spelling patterns.

Throughout the series, the texts provide the reader with the opportunity to practice and apply knowledge of the sounds in natural language. The books introduce sounds using familiar onsets and *rimes*, or spelling patterns, for reinforcement.

For example, the word *cat* might be used to present the short "a" sound, with the letter *c* being the onset and "_at" being the rime. This approach provides practice and reinforcement of the short "a" sound, as there are many familiar words made with the "_at" rime.

The stories and accompanying photographs in this series are based on time-honored concepts in children's literature: well-written, engaging texts and colorful, high-quality photographs combine to produce books that children want to read again and again.

Dr. Peg Ballard
Minnesota State University, Mankato

childsworld.com

Published by The Child's World®
1980 Lookout Drive • Mankato, MN 56003-1705
800-599-READ • www.childsworld.com

ACKNOWLEDGMENTS
The Child's World®: Mary Swensen, Publishing Director
The Design Lab: Design
Michael Miller: Editing

PHOTO CREDITS
© Africa Studio/Shutterstock.com: cover; Aonthip
Aorthong/Shutterstock.com: 10; chanus/Shutterstock.com:
9; Chonlawut/Shutterstock.com: 6; Enzart/Shutterstock.
com: 2; Fotokostic/Shutterstock.com: 18; Gucio_55/
Shutterstock.com: 5; HHelene/Shutterstock.com: 13;
holbox/Shutterstock.com: 21; Meister Photos/Shutterstock.
com: 14; sarawuth wannasathit/Shutterstock.com: 17

ISBN 9781503809116
LCCN 2015958463

Printed in the United States of America
Mankato, MN
June, 2016
PA02310

ABOUT THE AUTHOR

Alice K. Flanagan lives with her husband in Chicago, Illinois, and writes books for children and teachers. Ever since she was a young girl, Ms. Flanagan has enjoyed writing. Today, she has more than 70 books published on a wide variety of topics. Some of the books she has written include biographies of U.S. presidents and first ladies; biographies of people working in our neighborhoods; phonics books for beginning readers; informational books about birds; and career education in the classroom.